TRANSPORTATION
INVENTORS

by
Rebecca Phillips-Bartlett

Minneapolis, Minnesota

Credits

All images are courtesy of Shutterstock.com, unless otherwise specified. With thanks to Getty Images, Thinkstock Photo, and iStockphoto.

Recurring images – Andrew Rybalko, cosmaa, andromina, P-fotography, Mark Rademaker, IGORdeyka. Cover – Andrew Rybalko, dimair, cosmaa, andromina, P-fotography. 2–3 – Andrew Rybalko. 4–5 – IGORdeyka, Macrovector, Krakenimages.com. 6–7 – Naci Yavuz, Fourvierolim. 8–9 – Looper, Everett Collection, Serg_Zavyalov_photo. 10–11 – Lesseps, Magnus Manske, Irina Qiwi, AntiDeviL, J J Osuna Caballero. 12–13 – Flash Vector, Wiki LIC, klyaksun. 14–15 – shako, PixelSquid3d, Ann in the uk, Scewing. 16–17 – Nesnad, Chereliss, Foto-Ruhrgebiet, Flash Vector. 18–19 – JEFF KOWALSKY / Stringer, In-Finity, Real Vector, Valentina Sabelskaia. 20–21 – BlueBreezeWiki, Montbarrey, Morphart Creation, Panda Vector, PK Designs, ideyweb, Andrey Korzun. 22–23 – topseller.

Library of Congress Cataloging-in-Publication Data

Names: Phillips-Bartlett, Rebecca, 1999- author.
Title: Transportation inventors / by Rebecca Phillips-Bartlett.
Description: Minneapolis, MN : Bearport Publishing Company, [2024] |
   Series: Brilliant people, big ideas | Includes index.
Identifiers: LCCN 2023030978 (print) | LCCN 2023030979 (ebook) | ISBN
   9798889163596 (library binding) | ISBN 9798889163640 (paperback) | ISBN
   9798889163688 (ebook)
Subjects: LCSH: Transportation engineering--Juvenile literature. |
   Inventors--Juvenile literature. | Transportation--Juvenile literature. |
   CYAC: Transportation. | Inventors. | Transportation engineering.
Classification: LCC TA1149 .P483 2024 (print) | LCC TA1149 (ebook) | DDC
   629.04092--dc23/eng/20230713
LC record available at https://lccn.loc.gov/2023030978
LC ebook record available at https://lccn.loc.gov/2023030979

© 2024 BookLife Publishing
This edition is published by arrangement with BookLife Publishing.

North American adaptations © 2024 Bearport Publishing Company. All rights reserved. No part of this publication may be reproduced in whole or in part, stored in any retrieval system, or transmitted in any form or by any means, electronic, mechanical, photocopying, recording, or otherwise, without written permission from the publisher.

For more information, write to Bearport Publishing, 5357 Penn Avenue South, Minneapolis, MN 55419.

Contents

Big Ideas 4
Joseph-Michel and
 Jacques-Etienne Montgolfier ... 6
Richard Trevithick 8
Karl von Drais 10
Mary Anderson 12
Wilbur and Orville Wright 14
Garrett Morgan 16
Nils Bohlin 18
The Hall of Fame 20
All You Need Is an Idea! 22
Glossary 24
Index 24

Big Ideas

We travel all the time. In the past, traveling any distance was very hard. Now, transportation of all kinds helps people get around every day.

From bikes to airplanes, who do we have to thank for amazing moving **inventions**? These scientists and inventors turned big ideas into **brilliant** inventions.

What is your favorite way to travel?

Joseph-Michel and Jacques-Étienne Montgolfier

1740–1810

1745–1799

We wanted to be able to fly!

Hot-Air Balloons

French brothers Joseph-Michel and Jacques-Étienne Montgolfier noticed something about hot air. When they filled a bag with it, the bag would float up. This led to the creation of the hot-air balloon.

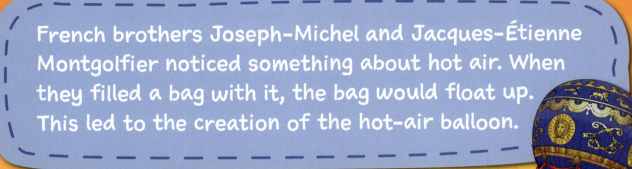

The brothers' first hot-air balloon flew about 3,000 feet (1,000 m) into the air for around 10 minutes.

Hot-air balloons were one of the first ways people took flight to explore the skies. This invention made traveling in the air possible.

Richard Trevithick

Horses are so slow and weak. There must be a better way to move heavy things....

1771–1833

Steam Engine

Richard Trevithick wanted an easier way to move people and heavy **cargo**. So, he invented the steam **engine** to power trains.

Richard's first train was nicknamed the Puffer.

At first, his steam engine was too heavy for the train **rails**. It took Richard a long time to get his invention to work.

Karl von Drais

1785–1851

Bikes

Karl von Drais invented a machine with a seat and two wheels. It looked like a bike, but it did not have **pedals**! Instead of pedaling, people pushed themselves along with their feet.

What would your dream bike look like?

Karl's bike was different from the ones we have today. Still, his invention is often thought of as the first bike.

Mary Anderson

There has to be a way to clean car windows without stopping....

1866–1953

Windshield Wipers

Mary Anderson noticed her driver had to keep stopping to wipe the windows in bad weather. So, she invented windshield wipers. These help drivers clean the windows from inside a car.

What is the weirdest thing you have seen out the car window?

Today, every car has windshield wipers. They help drivers see where they are going.

Wilbur and Orville Wright

Imagine if we could make a real-life flying machine....

1867–1912

1871–1948

Airplanes

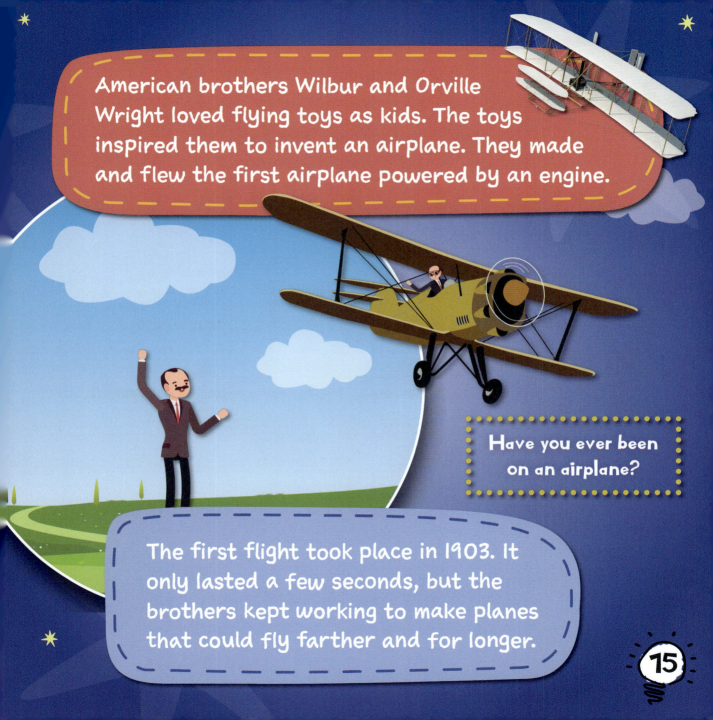

American brothers Wilbur and Orville Wright loved flying toys as kids. The toys inspired them to invent an airplane. They made and flew the first airplane powered by an engine.

Have you ever been on an airplane?

The first flight took place in 1903. It only lasted a few seconds, but the brothers kept working to make planes that could fly farther and for longer.

Garrett Morgan

"There must be a way to make driving safer...."

1877–1963

Traffic Signals

Traffic signals used to have only two colors that told drivers to stop or go. Garret Morgan added another light to warn people that the light was changing. It gave them time to slow down.

If you designed a traffic signal, what colors would you choose?

The traffic signals we see today still use Garrett's idea. His invention has made roads safer and saved many lives.

Nils Bohlin

Most cars do not have seat belts. This does not seem very safe!

1920–2002

Seat Belts

Early seat belts had many problems, and not all cars had them. Nils Bohlin wanted to change this. He invented seat belts that are like the ones we use today.

Nils's three-point seat belt protected both a person's upper and lower body.

It took many years for his invention to become popular. People were not used to wearing seat belts and did not understand why seat belts were important. Today, we can all buckle up thanks to Nils!

19

The Hall of Fame

Here are some more brilliant people who deserve a place in our transportation hall of fame.

Claude de Jouffroy d'Abbans

1751-1832

Claude de Jouffroy d'Abbans made the first successful steamboat. The boat made it easier to travel long distances across the ocean.

Karl Friedrich Benz

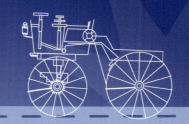

It took many brilliant people to invent the cars we use today. Karl Friedrich Benz was one of these people. He came up with a better kind of engine.

1844-1929

Sergei Korolev

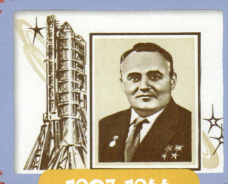

Sergei Korolev invented many amazing spacecraft. He even invented the one that sent the first person into space!

1907-1966

All You Need Is an Idea!

All these inventions started the same way. They were big ideas. From hot-air balloons to seat belts, many of our favorite ways to travel wouldn't be the same without these brilliant people.

They were trying to solve problems. Traveling was too slow, cost too much money, or was not very safe. These inventors worked hard to change the way we travel today.

What would you invent to make traveling better?

23

Glossary

brilliant extremely smart

cargo a load of goods or supplies

engine a machine that uses energy to make things go

inventions new things that have been made to solve problems

pedals foot levers used to make bikes go

rails steel bars that form a train track

traffic cars on a road

Index

airplanes 5, 14–15
bikes 5, 10–11
cars 12–13, 18–19, 21
horses 8, 10
hot-air balloons 6–7, 22
seat belts 18–19, 22

spacecraft 21
steamboats 20
steam engines 8–9
traffic signals 16–17
windshield wipers 12–13